# Louis XIV

*J. H. Shennan*

METHUEN · LONDON

First published in 1986 by
Methuen & Co. Ltd
11 New Fetter Lane
London EC4P 4EE

© 1986 J. H. Shennan

Typeset in Great Britain by
Scarborough Typesetting Services
and printed by
Richard Clay (The Chaucer Press)
Bungay, Suffolk

British Library Cataloguing in
Publication Data

Shennan, J. H.
Louis XIV. – (Lancaster pamphlets)
1. France – History –
Louis XIV, 1643–1715
I. Title   II. Series
944'.033    DC125

ISBN 0–416–37340–2

# Contents

# Foreword

Lancaster Pamphlets offer concise and up-to-date accounts of major historical topics, primarily for the help of students preparing for Advanced Level examinations, though they should also be of value to those pursuing introductory courses in universities and other institutions of higher education. They do not rely on prior textbook knowledge. Without being all-embracing, their aims are to bring some of the central themes or problems confronting students and teachers into sharper focus than the textbook writer can hope to do; to provide the reader with some of the results of recent research which the textbook may not embody; and to stimulate thought about the whole interpretation of the topic under discussion.

At the end of this pamphlet is a list of the recent or fairly recent works that the writer considers most relevant to the subject.

Europe in 1715

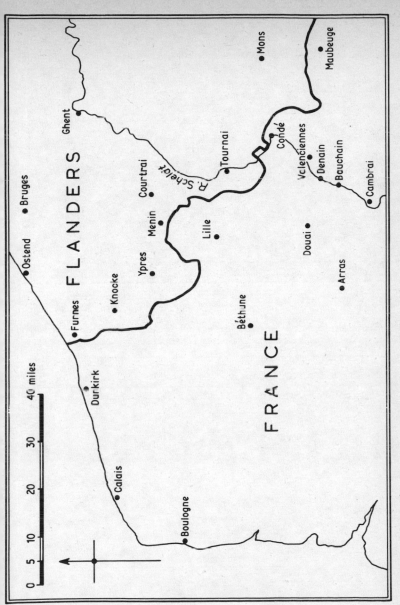

France's north-eastern frontier

# Louis XIV

## Prologue

The future Louis XIV was born at the royal château of Saint-Germain on 5 September 1638. He was the first child of King Louis XIII and of Anne of Austria, who, despite her title, was a Spanish princess, the daughter of King Philip III. In 1643, while still a young child, he succeeded his father as King of France and he reigned until 1715, dying just four days before his seventy-seventh birthday.

These brief biographical details contain the key to two of the most significant factors to be considered when assessing the reign of Louis XIV. First, there is the matter of its sheer length. No other reign in modern European history lasted so long and we need to bear in mind that over such a lengthy period the king's attitudes and policies were likely to undergo modification and change. Only a singularly insensitive or stupid man – and Louis was neither – could have remained immune to changing circumstances and ideas as his reign stretched on into the generation of his great-grandchildren. Although we will shortly consider those influences and principles which shaped his basic outlook, we should not overlook the fundamental importance of his longevity.

The second key factor concerns Louis's family or dynastic connections. That Louis's ancestral blood relations were more Habsburg than Bourbon is often overlooked. He was descended from a line of great European princes which included Charles the Bold of Burgundy, the Medici Lorenzo the Magnificent of Florence, the Emperor Charles V, and Philip II of Spain, the last his great-grandfather. The effect of this impressive lineage was to make Louis perceive Europe in a fashion very different from that of later rulers. Whereas modern governments

1

concentrate their attention exclusively upon their own well-defined sovereign areas or states, Louis took a wider view of the European continent. There were few areas which had not concerned his family at some point in the past and many in which the king retained a residual interest.

This dynastic rather than national outlook helps to throw light upon Louis's relations with the Habsburg powers in Germany and Spain. It is also a salutary reminder of the fact that both international relations and domestic politics in the age of Louis XIV were based upon criteria which were fundamentally different in kind from those to which we have now become accustomed.

## Influences upon the king

Bearing these twin considerations in mind we can proceed to examine the particular influences which helped to mould Louis XIV's kingship.

### RELIGION

The French king inherited with his crown the title of Most Christian Majesty. Upon his accession he was anointed with holy oil in a ceremony which not only confirmed his status as the leading layman in France but also made him the country's leading ecclesiastical figure. Though not a cleric himself, he was entitled to preside over the council of the French Church, and to legislate as its head on matters concerning its relations with the secular power and with the Papacy. The evident sign of his God-given authority was the royal claim to possess miraculous powers of healing. These the French king ceremoniously exercised on the great feast days of the year, by touching subjects afflicted with 'the King's Evil' or scrofula, a distressing skin complaint.

By the time of Louis XIV's accession the doctrine of the divine right of kings had become firmly established in the wake of the civil wars of religion at the end of the previous century. The assassination of two of Louis's predecessors, Henry III and Henry IV, ironically bolstered the authority of kingship. In the interests of peace and stability subjects preferred to believe that the monarchy was inseparable from the divinity and that no power on earth could challenge the one without affronting the other. This doctrine further distanced the monarchy from the people, though the religious connotations of the royal office had for a long time created an awesome image for the king of France.

2

Louis XIV never underestimated the importance of religion to his kingship. Indeed, it contributed an inherent element in his public life. This was despite the indiscretions and scandals which characterized what later generations would call his private life.

But the fact was that the king had no private life. He chose to make himself a public institution, providing a constant focus of respect and loyalty for his subjects, the very embodiment of his state. Thus during the heyday of the royal mistresses, the decades of the sixties and seventies, when the king was in the prime of his life, Louis's tangled relations with 'the three queens', Maria Theresa, his first wife, and his two most famous mistresses, Louise de la Vallière and the Marquise de Montespan, preoccupied the court and the king's advisers. Indeed, such is human nature that they provoked rather more interest in Paris than the events of the War of Devolution and the Dutch War, both of which were fought during this period. The king's decision not to take communion during the Easter of 1664 because of his liaison with La Vallière, and his temporary separation from Montespan in 1675 following pressure from his Jesuit confessor, Father de la Chaise, and the formidable court preacher and writer, Bishop Bossuet, were public acts with political implications. In particular, they invited a judgment upon Louis's performance as God's lieutenant, as ruler of France by divine right.

Nobody was surprised that, in a world of arranged royal marriages, the king should take a mistress. The tradition was long established and some of the most distinguished names at court, like the Vendôme, were descended from an illicit liaison. However, Louis's double adultery with the married Madame de Montespan caused particular scandal and the king himself eventually recognized the need to behave with more circumspection.

During the last three and a half decades of his reign his court became a far more discreet and sober place, with ultimately an air of gloomy introspection, reminiscent of the court of his Spanish great-grandfather, Philip II. We will consider later the influence of his second wife, Madame de Maintenon, in effecting this transformation which began with the king's permanent move to his newly restructured palace of Versailles. There can be no doubt, however, that the disasters of the War of the Spanish Succession, the final war of Louis's reign, and especially the loss within twelve months in 1711–12 of three heirs to the throne and one much loved granddaughter-in-law, Marie Adelaide, duchess of Burgundy, filled the stoical old king with a sadness which remained with him until his death.

3

Louis was not a man of deep spiritual fervour, even in his last years. He was a conventional Christian who accepted the obligations of his religion as naturally as he breathed, and with as little questioning or analysis. Every morning he attended mass as part of the day's ritual. He played his part in the great ceremonial occasions of the Church's year and issued regulations to the court prohibiting the eating of meat during Lent. His confessors had just as important a role in the king's entourage as his secular advisers, the ministers of state who attended his council. Even the prestigious military confraternities, the Order of the Holy Spirit and the Order of St Michael, were shot through with religious connotations and ceremonial.

There existed, therefore, in Louis XIV's world an acceptance of the fact that man must ultimately answer to God for his actions in this world. Kings were not exempt from this final inquisition; indeed, their power on earth was such as to increase their responsibility in the sight of God who would expect more of his earthly lieutenants than of humbler souls. It was in the king's interest, therefore, to act in a Christian manner towards his subjects, if he were not to risk eternal damnation. It is important, though difficult, for later generations with a very different outlook to appreciate the power of this sanction in influencing royal actions.

### THE LAW

The king of France was his country's chief judge. His primary obligation had always been that of dispensing justice to his subjects, originally in person and later through his courts. The king's residual authority to judge in person was retained in the mechanism of the *lit de justice*, a ceremony which allowed him to overturn the opinions of the chief magistrates of his kingdom. He could also permit the right of appeal to the royal council. Thus, in addition to his duty to respect the laws of God, Louis XIV inherited an obligation to honour the secular law which gave France order and stability. He remained the absolute ruler of his kingdom, which meant that no individual or institution could challenge his supreme power, but he was also expected to uphold the authority of the laws which he had inherited with his kingdom as well as to amend outmoded legislation and create new laws when necessary. This was the meaning of the famous distinction made by Bossuet between absolute and arbitrary power. The bishop believed that the latter – which was the exercise of authority without recourse to

4

established legal principles – was not acceptable in France, though it might be thought suitable in Moscow or in Constantinople.

The strength of the king's judicial authority grew out of the legitimacy of his own succession. According to French law, the rightful king was invariably the predecessor's eldest male heir in the direct legitimate line. Louis XIV conformed to this fundamental rule. Having answered a legal summons to the throne, therefore, he was entitled to give the law to his subjects.

Yet the legal constraints under which the king was expected to rule did not prevent him, on occasion, from acting in defiance of the law. Since there was no institutional curb on his authority it was tempting to do so from time to time. Thus, very near the end of his reign, in July 1714, Louis declared his two illegitimate sons by Madame de Montespan, the Duke du Maine and the Count de Toulouse, capable of succeeding to the crown in the event of the failure of the legitimate line. He was driven to take this step by the series of deaths in the royal family which has already been mentioned, by the death of a second grandson in 1714, and by the accession to the Spanish throne of Philip V, his remaining grandson, who was forced to renounce his rights to the French crown at the Peace of Utrecht. It appeared possible that the royal line would be extinguished and Louis was prepared to take desperate measures to prevent such an event. However, there was no precedent for the succession to the French throne of an illegitimate son, and Louis must have known that he was flouting one of the most fundamental of French laws.

Similarly, at about the same time, he tried to impose the papal bull *Unigenitus* upon the French Church, even though a part of its content and the procedure he adopted were at odds with the Gallican Articles which he himself had been instrumental in extracting from the Pope in 1682. Towards the end of his long life, Louis's anxiety to crush the unorthodox religious movement known as Jansenism, and thereby improve his prospects of eternal salvation, led him to discount the dubious legality of his actions. In both these cases it may well be that an old man, long accustomed to power and deference, lost patience with legal niceties in the face of what he considered to be more pressing considerations.

Despite such glaring examples of arbitrary action, historians in recent years have been inclined to give Louis XIV credit for generally abiding by the rule of law. They point out for example that the use of royal *lettres de cachet*, which allowed the king to imprison subjects without

5

reference to the courts, was generally employed not as a political weapon but on behalf of heads of families anxious to control their wayward children. Again, in 1710, when the king was at war and desperately short of funds, he hesitated to introduce a new Tenth tax until he had consulted lawyers of the Sorbonne to discover whether they thought he was entitled to do so. They decided that he was, and the tax was duly introduced. But, like the Capitation tax of 1695, it was intended to be only a temporary wartime expedient. This was because both taxes trespassed upon the traditional legal immunities of privileged groups.

Historians have also revised their views of the various law-codes promulgated during the reign: the civil code (1667), the criminal code (1670), the maritime code (1672), the commercial code (1673) and the Black Code of 1685 dealing with the rights of slaves in the French colonies. They now appear as monuments to a new humanitarian spirit and not simply as a means to concentrate power in royal hands. These codifications did, of course, strengthen the authority of royal government, though it is arguable that the king's traditional obligation to dispense justice in person gave him the right to superimpose his law over a multitude of conflicting local customs. That argument applies not only to the central administration of justice, but also to the powers of the intendants who represented the king's authority in the provinces.

Finally, in the context of reason of state (to which we must return later), it is possible to maintain that the king's sovereign responsibilities sometimes forced him to suspend normal legal procedures. For example, in 1673 he forbade the *Parlement* of Paris, his chief law-court, to remonstrate against proposed legislation until after it had been registered. By this means he ensured the prompt execution of new laws, including those concerning finance, an important consideration during the emergency created by the Dutch War (1672–8/9) (see p. 35). It is true that he succeeded in extending that state of emergency, and consequently of *parlementaire* impotence, until the end of his reign. On the other hand, his recognition of the court's right of remonstrance and his continued insistence upon the importance of registering royal acts in the *Parlement* testify to his respect for traditional law-making procedures.

Louis XIV's conduct in relation to the law was not guiltless. Nor is it surprising that in the course of a long, unfettered reign he should succumb from time to time to the temptations of power. Yet the traditional judicial nature of his authority and the pressing obligations of reason of state together justified much that contemporaries and later historians found indefensible. Louis was capable of breaking the law, but not of denying its existence.

### THE FAMILY

Louis XIV was the proud head of a great European family, the Bourbons, and dynastic considerations always figured prominently in his political calculations. In his so-called Memoirs, which were in fact instructions written for the son who was destined not to outlive him, he referred to this line of 'hereditary kings who can boast that there isn't either a better house, nor greater power, nor more absolute authority than theirs anywhere else in the world'.

On one level he interpreted his kingship in the proprietorial terms of land-ownership. France was the family's inheritance, whose possession entailed responsibilities as well as privileges. Much has been made by historians of Louis's quest for glory. That aspect of his reign should not be judged merely in terms of ostentatious military grandeur or the cult of the royal personality, despite an air of arrogance about the régime. For there was more to it than that. Louis believed that he was obliged to hand on to his successor a state at least as rich, honoured and secure as that which he had inherited from his father. That was the stimulus for the pursuit of *gloire*: it was a matter of family honour as much as of personal self-glorification.

In particular, like many estate-owning country gentlemen, he had to ensure that the boundaries of his land were properly secured so that trespassers could not invade at will and damage his property. He also had an obligation to his tenants to see that they were not disturbed by such incursions, as well as to treat them justly and in a Christian manner. It is easy to see how such fundamental obligations could be extended in the course of a long reign. The acquisition of additional territories might seem justified as a means of guaranteeing the country's frontiers from attack, for example. But were the costs of the resulting wars a justified burden for the subjects to bear? This is one of the important questions underlying the consideration of Louis's foreign policy.

It was sometimes difficult to distinguish between Louis's role as head of the Bourbon house and as king of France. The king's deeply felt sense of family ownership can be illustrated by reference to the great palace of Versailles outside Paris, where for the last three decades of his reign

Louis established both his home and the centre of his government. His great bedchamber was deliberately sited at the very centre of the re-designed palace to symbolize the king's position at the heart of his kingdom. It was the daily focal point of elaborate ceremonial designed to instil a sense of awe into the subjects' minds. Yet it was also the master bedroom of the château's owner where close relatives and friends were received, where in fact the king finally died in 1715. Literally next door was the council chamber where decisions were taken by the king and his chief advisers which concerned not the rituals of the palace but matters of war and peace throughout Europe and overseas. It was not considered necessary to separate the location of one royal activity from another, or one group of the king's intimates from another. Thus ministers and courtiers rubbed shoulders with princes and with the king's own children. The patriarchal Louis expected the latter to live with their families under his own roof so that the unity of the kingdom would not be weakened by the establishment of an alternative court. He was extremely displeased when his only legitimate son, Louis *le grand dauphin*, set up home at the château of Meudon, several miles to the east of Versailles.

Stepping outside into the splendid gardens of Versailles which were designed by Le Nôtre as an integral part of the palace's embellishment, we observe the same confusion between the king's personal and public role. His pride in the gardens was that of a country gentleman, pre-occupied with ordering and cultivating his favourite flowers (heliotrope and orange blossom), overseeing the herbs and vegetables, busying him-self with the pruning and pollination of his apple and pear trees. He even wrote a guide to the gardens and led his own conducted tours. At the same time, on the other side of the great façade, a new building was being added to the palace to accommodate ministerial offices, staffs and records, another reminder of the fact that his country estate was the hub of French government as well as the king's favourite residence.

This growing professionalism, which characterized Louis XIV's kingship as much as his proprietory sense, stems from early family influences, those exercised by his mother, the Regent, Queen Anne, and by his godfather, the Italian-born Cardinal Mazarin. The two worked closely together though the view once held that they had secretly married some time after Louis XIII's death is not now widely held. The Cardinal was in official charge of the young king's education and he considered his brief to include responsibility for developing Louis's understanding of his political obligations.

Mazarin introduced the king to the practical matters of statecraft, the way in which council meetings should be managed, the dispatches from the many French ambassadors and representatives interpreted, and instructions drafted. By the age of sixteen Louis was spending at least two hours a day with the Cardinal learning how to take political decisions. His mother, whom Louis resembled physically, instilled into the king the virtues of hard work and patience in carrying out the responsibilities imposed by his office, characteristics reminiscent again of her Spanish grandfather, Philip II. Louis XIV grew up, therefore, with an idea of kingship as being something more than dynastic inheritance. It was certainly that, but it also demanded a high level of professional expertise. Being king of France was no occupation for an amateur.

If the Queen Mother and Cardinal Mazarin were the chief influences upon the king in the early years of his reign, his second wife, Madame de Maintenon, was the dominating figure during his declining years. There was a significant difference, however, between her influence and that of Anne and Mazarin. Whereas Mazarin in particular played a formal part in shaping his political attitudes, Maintenon's hold over the king was private and informal. When Louis met his future second wife (they married secretly during the 1680s), he had been in absolute command of government for a long time. It would have been unthinkable for him to allow her to interfere directly in affairs of state. Behind the scenes, however, she became the recipient of the king's confidences and privy to the discussions between her husband and his advisers. Indeed, Louis acquired the habit of holding important ministerial meetings in her rooms.

The extent of her influence behind any of the important political decisions taken by the king, especially after 1700, remains a matter for debate. She may have pushed him to make a will advantageous to her own favourite among Louis's illegitimate children, the Duke du Maine, whose nurse she had been during the days of Madame de Montespan's supremacy at court. The same pressure may have lurked behind Louis's misguided declaration, already referred to, that permitted Maine and his younger brother, the Count de Toulouse, to succeed to the throne in the absence of legitimate heirs. However, we cannot be sure, and the fact that Maine was also a favourite of the king underlines the element of uncertainty.

We are on firmer ground when considering Maintenon's influence upon the king's religious attitudes. He himself acknowledged her

9

efforts to translate his conventional and superficial approach into a more genuine fervour. Even in this matter, however, we should remember that Louis, saddened by military defeats and by the deaths in his close family, and conscious of his own mortality, was a more pliant subject than he would have been in earlier, triumphant years.

One final point may be made about Madame de Maintenon. She should not be perceived as simply a woman of deep religious convictions. No resident of Louis XIV's Versailles has been so consistently underestimated by historians as the ruler's second wife. The simple fact that she overcame her birth in a debtor's prison, the daughter of an impoverished petty nobleman, to marry a king of France preoccupied with his family's prestige, is testimony enough to the formidable personality of this handsome and intelligent woman.

### THE FRONDES

Louis XIV's childhood was marred by two civil wars lasting from 1648 to 1652. They were known as the *Frondes* from the French word for the sling or catapult with which Parisian children fought their street battles. The impact of these wars upon the young king, who at one stage was forced to flee from his own capital, made them the most significant episode of his life. His experience during the *Frondes* provided the thrust for many of his later policies and shaped his attitude to subjects in high places. The issue at the heart of this series of civil disturbances was whether central government, represented in Louis XIV's minority by the Queen and the Cardinal, had the right to make legislative decisions without regard either to the great princes of the blood who had once been the natural advisers of the king or to the chief law-court in the land, the *Parlement* of Paris.

The latter's long-standing claim to play a constitutional role in approving or rejecting royal enactments was boosted during the years of the 1640s by events in England, even though there were fundamental differences between that body and the English Parliament. This basic argument about the nature of French government had been in progress for many generations. It burst into life at the beginning of Louis's reign partly because minorities were always periods of royal weakness and partly because Mazarin, as a foreigner, was a convenient scapegoat who could be attacked with impunity.

In general, Louis XIV's reaction to the *Frondes* later in his reign was to pursue and tighten up those policies of central government organization and control which he believed offered the best means of thwarting rebellion. To some extent this policy was at the expense of customary local rights and liberties though, as we have already seen, there were other strong pressures on Louis which militated against the arbitrary imposition of royal power.

In more particular respects, too, Louis's attitudes during his majority reflected his experience during the *Frondes*. His mistrust of the great nobles who had been able to take up arms against his government was matched by a determination to build a powerful royal army strong enough to prevent the crown from being further humiliated by its overmighty subjects. He never trusted the judges of his supreme court of *Parlement* either, nor any group who seemed capable of dividing the kingdom. He wanted conformity, religious as well as political, and above all he wanted order: order in the social hierarchy, which was pushed almost to caricature in the rules governing conduct at Versailles; order in the substitution of a highly trained bureaucratically organized royal army for the uncertain loyalty of the feudal levy; order in the capital where the first lieutenant-general of police, appointed in 1667, instituted a system of street-lighting to reduce the high level of violence at night; order in the arts and sciences by means of the royal foundation of a series of academies, of painting and sculpture, architecture, sciences and inscriptions, to regulate these activities in a manner likely to add lustre to the king's state. There was much in Louis XIV's France which strikes modern observers as highly disorganized, but which had no such effect on the king who was no less a prisoner of his age than any other human being. Yet his desire for a greater degree of regulation and control than many of his contemporaries thought proper should be noted. So should the fact that this policy, though not a novel one, was given considerable impetus as a result of the young king's experiences during the *Frondes*.

We must conclude this section on a negative note. It used to be argued that the king's decision to quit Paris for Versailles was made as a result of unhappy childhood memories of Parisian disloyalty and violence during the *Frondes*. This hypothesis is no longer generally accepted for it is only tenable if we telescope the events of Louis's long reign. It must be remembered that he did not move permanently to Versailles until 1682, thirty years after the end of the civil wars.

# Domestic policy

France under Louis XIV was governed by a conciliar system. If we look closely at this system of councils we can learn a great deal about some of the most important features of the reign.

There is often confusion about the number of royal councils existing at this time. In fact, there was only one, the King's Council. Had there been more than one the unique authority of the king would have been threatened by the possibility of division. The confusion has been due to the fact that the council met under a series of different names in order to deal with differing kinds of business. The personnel changed too, according to the type of session, but all were royal councillors and all the sessions were deemed to be meetings of the royal council because their authority depended upon the King. However, the number of titles under which the royal council met fluctuated over the course of the reign. There were four which had a continuous existence: the High Council, the Council for the Interior or the Despatches, the Royal Council of Finance and the Privy Council. The king always chaired the first three and though he did not attend the Privy Council, an empty armchair symbolized that it too was a meeting of the royal council.

The High Council was the king's chief committee. It was concerned with all important matters of state, though it tended increasingly to concentrate on foreign affairs. Its membership was very small, between three and five councillors. These were the ministers of state about whom it is worth making several observations. Nobody sat by right, or by virtue of his office, at the High Council. The title of minister depended upon the king's summons and if he ceased to call a particular adviser that individual at once ceased to be a minister.

Thus the absolute authority of the king was reconciled with the obligation traditionally accepted by his predecessors to take counsel. Louis expressed both aspects of royal authority in advising his grandson (who in 1700 became King Philip V of Spain) to listen to his Council but then to take the final decisions himself. Louis believed that professional advice had to be taken seriously, but he also believed that his vocation as king by divine right gave him an additional wisdom and insight which justified his having the last word.

Louis's ministers were more professional than their predecessors. No longer could members of the royal family, princes of the blood, representatives of great noble dynasties, expect to be summoned to advise the king simply because they were who they were. Instead, the king looked to his controller-general of finance and to his secretaries of state, experts in the fields of administration and diplomacy, in military and naval affairs.

These ministers have sometimes been misleadingly described as middle-class, a misapprehension which can be traced to the hostility expressed against these powerful new figures by members of the high nobility who had lost their political influence. Louis was too conscious of rank and dignity ever to employ non-nobles in such high offices of state. Their very position as royal councillors guaranteed them nobility, though in fact their background was of the minor nobility. Having acquired such distinction in the king's service, his councillors, particularly his ministers, could expect their families to rise rapidly in the social hierarchy. Though the father of Louis's great minister, Colbert, was an undistinguished petty nobleman from Rheims, all his granddaughters married dukes.

Louis appointed only seventeen ministers in the course of his long reign and most of them belonged to or were connected by marriage with one of three families, the Colbert, the Le Tellier and the Phély-peaux. In addition, a total of five secretaries of state who did not achieve ministerial rank came from the latter two families. They were not all of equal ability, but where else should the king look for his chief servants if not to those families which had demonstrated their total commitment to his cause, in which sons and grandsons grew up apprenticed to his service? He valued their expertise in the task of making central government more effective and he was surer of their loyalty than he had been of the loyalty of an earlier generation of great men surrounding his throne. There was one notable absentee from the High Council: the office of First Minister was not filled after Mazarin's death. Though Louis had been genuinely fond of his godfather, he never forgot how attacks on the first minister during the *Frondes* had weakened royal authority. After the Cardinal's death in 1661 he decided to be his own first minister.

The Council for the Interior received reports from the king's agents in the provinces and sent out its own instructions in response. Its membership was a little larger than that of the High Council including, besides the king, the chancellor, the secretaries of state and the controller-general of finance. This latter figure was a key member of the small Royal Council of Finance which was responsible both for broad economic and financial policy and for detailed accounting and book-keeping.

The Privy Council had quite a different appearance from the three government councils so far discussed. The king himself was absent and the chair was taken by his chief legal officer, the chancellor. The council's personnel consisted of several dozen lawyers, for its primary function was judicial, that of deciding cases withdrawn from the juris-diction of the ordinary courts. As the organization of government had gradually grown more complex the crown had created a series of law courts through which judicial authority would normally be exercised. Yet kings retained the power to dispense personal justice to their subjects, a power which in Louis XIV's reign was invested in the Privy Council. It provided the king with a means of reinforcing that central government control which had proved to be so vulnerable during the *Frondes*. However, if the king persistently circumvented his own courts he risked being accused of despotism, thereby under-mining his own legal authority. That risk would become a serious problem for Louis's successor in his relations with the *Parlement* of Paris.

In formal terms, then, the central government was run by the king in conjunction with his councils. Louis had learned his professionalism from Mazarin and throughout his life he devoted a number of hours a day on most days of the week to the routines of administration. The conciliar system affirmed the responsible nature of his authority with-out challenging its absolute character. However, subtle modifications were being introduced which promised to strengthen the power of central government but at the cost of making it appear irresponsible or arbitrary. Roland Mousnier's description of the conciliar system as 'a magnificent façade' exaggerates the position but draws attention to the need to look closely at what was happening behind the scenes.

First and foremost, government was becoming more bureaucratic. The increased professionalism to which we have drawn attention did not stop with the king and his chief councillors. Records had to be kept and officials appointed to advise the king's advisers. Such changes threatened to undermine the traditional character of the government which required the king to be viewed as his country's chief judge, not its chief administrator. There was a legality about the former role which was not necessarily to be found in the latter. That would seem particu-larly so if the administrative processes were to become detached from the normally accepted procedures.

A sign that this development was beginning to take place can be observed in the changing roles of the chancellor and the controller-general of finance. As the king's chief judicial expert, the former had long played a leading part in government, even deputizing for the king as chairman of the Royal Council. Under Louis XIV, however, the office lost much of its effective authority. The chancellor was not even an ex-officio member of the Royal Council for Finance, though previously chancellors had figured prominently in the administration of the king's finances. There were of course no ex-officio members of the High Council. Louis only summoned those chancellors to attend who were already ministers of state.

As the office of chancellor lost political importance so that of controller-general acquired new significance. He became the effective head of the financial administration of the country and of all aspects of the economy. Indeed, it would not be an exaggeration to claim that he acquired overall responsibility for domestic affairs. He took over from the chancellor, for example, the task of nominating the provincial intendants, thereby pushing his authority over a wide range of affairs deep into the localities.

Nor was that the limit of the controller-general's new-found influence. Many important matters were decided privately in discussions between the king and the controller-general and then formally approved in council. Two highly significant financial edicts, the Capitation (1695) and the Tenth (1710), both of which incorporated the novel principle of taxing privileged and non-privileged subjects alike, were handled in this way. The controller-general's bureau became a centre of expertise which no outsider could fully comprehend and control. For form's sake its decisions were sometimes pushed through the conciliar system, but sometimes they acquired executive force simply by virtue of the controller-general's signature on behalf of the king.

The growth in importance of the post of controller-general provides the best evidence of a significant but subtle shift in the nature of government under Louis XIV which would become apparent after his death. Despite the survival of the conciliar system, based upon the king's primacy as a judge, a new administrative régime was beginning to take shape alongside it. This new order made for greater central government control because of the relative speed and efficiency with which business could be despatched. It also provided the king with one formidable agent in the person of the controller-general who yet remained a royal creature. For although the secretaries of state and most of the other

15

members of the royal council (though not the chancellor, who was appointed by the king for life) had been allowed to buy, inherit and bequeath their offices, thereby acquiring a degree of independence from government control, the function of the controller-general remained a commission dependent entirely upon the king's pleasure. The importance of the role played by Louis's most famous minister, Jean-Baptiste Colbert, in the expansion of the powers of this commission will be examined in a subsequent section.

### THE ADMINISTRATION OF THE PROVINCES

The most important provincial official during Louis XIV's reign was the intendant, whose increasing influence in the localities had been one of the causes of the *Frondes*. The intendant was a particularly effective agent of central government because of the extreme range and flexibility of his powers. His title, *l'intendant de police, justice et finances*, indicated that there were no matters of domestic policy beyond his reach. Like the controller-general, the intendant was a royal commissioner, unable to purchase his office and therefore directly dependent upon the king's continued support. The commission itself, which could be revoked at any time, enumerated the tasks of the intendant and the status of his decisions, whether, for example, they were subject to appeal in the supreme courts or only in the King's Council. These instructions were frequently modified or extended by subsequent council decrees. The government was therefore able to employ the intendants both in a broad supervisory capacity and to deal with particular matters. The latter might be the organization of a new tax, like the Capitation of 1695, or the implementation of an important piece of legislation, like the Edict of Fontainebleau (1685) which revoked the Edict of Nantes and led to the persecution of the French Protestants.

The most important area of the intendants' activities was that of finance. Indeed, their rise to pre-eminence in the years before the *Frondes* was primarily as fund raisers to enable France to remain at war. Though France was a rich country the crown experienced great difficulty in raising the financial resources which were needed to maintain security in wartime. That was for two reasons.

First, Frenchmen did not see themselves, nor did the government see them, as automatically obliged to take on that burden. France was a patchwork of regions and social groups, each with its own inherited relationship with central government, including its own financial rights and obligations. For example, the *pays d'état*, those provinces like Burgundy and Brittany which retained their own provincial assemblies, were taxed on a different footing from the remaining regions, the *pays d'élections*. The nobility and the clergy were exempt from the sole direct tax, the *taille*, yet in some regions the tax was levied on noblemen who owned land which had been classified as non-noble. The organizational problem of coping with such a complicated and unwieldy structure would have been formidable for the most efficient and dedicated civil service. But there was no such civil service available to Louis XIV.

This brings us to the second reason for the crown's financial difficulties, the inadequacy of the mechanisms available to bring in the dues to which the crown was entitled. For indirect taxes, a system of tax-farming operated whereby the king sold the right to collect taxes on a wide range of goods and services to individuals who were able to give him a lump sum in exchange. Invariably the crown lost revenue through this procedure. In 1699, for example, less than half of the indirect taxes raised by the largest syndicate, the so-called General Farm, went to the crown. The collection of the direct tax, the *taille*, was also grossly inefficient, for most of the crown's financial agents were office-holders who, having bought their office as an investment for themselves and their families, were not necessarily competent to carry out their responsibilities as tax-collectors. In times of emergency the king was forced to connive at this state of affairs by selling offices to raise money which he could not obtain in a more orthodox fashion.

The intendant, who had no independent interest and carried precise yet wide-ranging authorization from the king, made the government's voice more effective in the provinces. He supervised the allocation and collection of the *taille* in his district, which was called a *généralité*, examining any claims for exemption, checking that all those who should pay had done so, and that the collection was honestly conducted. He was also responsible for ensuring that the various tax-farmers acted in accordance with the government's decrees. Outside the sphere of taxation, the intendants were active in matters of military discipline, recruitment and supplies, in monitoring the price of food, inspecting weights and measures, checking the cleanliness of the streets, inspecting prisons, even imposing the death penalty in criminal cases brought before them.

What is striking about this list, which is by no means exhaustive, is the lack of any distinction under the *ancien régime* between justice and administration. We are once again reminded of the fact that the king's

17

authority was essentially judicial, and remained so even when delegated to the various administrators who served him. In the case of the intendants, however, as of the controller-general, the administrative element loomed larger than ever before, particularly since they too began to collect a considerable staff of secretaries and other officials. Such an increase in administrative activity, when supported by judicial authority, could threaten the interests of many groups and individuals in the localities. Louis XIV's instincts were deeply conservative, however. He had no wish to destroy the complex mosaic of laws, privileges and customs which he had inherited. He simply wanted to maximize his authority within the framework of the existing order. Consequently, Louis did not wish the intendants to take the place of the local courts and officials. He preferred their role to be investigative wherever possible, with reference back to the royal council before action was taken. We must beware of using hindsight to perceive the emergence of bureaucratic government before contemporaries had envisaged any such thing.

The intendants were noblemen of the new professional kind, the *noblesse de robe*. They were educated in the law and came usually from the ranks of the *maîtres des requêtes*, senior magistrates who also served in the King's Council. Their background differed therefore from that of the provincial governors who were longer-established representatives of the king in the provinces and were drawn from the old military and princely nobility. The office of governor fell into disfavour with the king as a result of the governors' activities during the *Frondes*, and from 1661 they were appointed only for a limited period. The office became increasingly honorific and its holders spent most of their time at court.

The new nobility, then, was ousting the old in provincial government, if not in high society, and in 1667 that tendancy was dramatically demonstrated. In that year Colbert ordered the intendants to investigate family titles to nobility. Consequently, proof of noble status would no longer depend upon private papers or local reputation but upon a legal, government-approved document entitled the *ordonnance de maintenir de noblesse*. The government wanted to know who was escaping taxation by claiming noble privilege. Louis himself was happy to tighten his grip upon a social group whose recent record of loyalty had been mixed.

## PERSONALITIES AND POLICIES

The most significant group of ministers summoned by Louis to assist at his High Council was the one assembled at the beginning of his personal

18

reign in 1661. In September of that year Fouquet, Louis's superintendant of finance, was dismissed on charges of peculation and subsequently imprisoned for life. From that time the king came to rely upon three men: Jean-Baptiste Colbert, Michel le Tellier and Hugues de Lionne. Along with Louis himself, this *triade*, as they were collectively known, developed a range of initiatives which would remain government policy for a number of years to come. Lionne's contribution was exclusively in the field of diplomacy and can be assessed best in the context of foreign affairs.

### Jean-Baptiste Colbert

Colbert is the best known of all Louis XIV's advisers. He epitomized the new type of official, hard-working and dedicated, who thrived under the patronage of the king. Before entering Louis's service he had been in charge of the organization of Mazarin's household, and the Cardinal himself had recommended him to his master. Born in 1619, he was almost twice the young king's age in 1661 when he was first invited to sit at the High Council. Thereafter he became superintendant of the king's buildings in 1664, controller-general of finance in the following year, and secretary of state for the marine in 1669. Though he left his mark on many areas of public life, he is most closely identified with the reorganization of the country's finances.

It would be wrong to describe Colbert's views as radical in any of the areas with which he was concerned. In financial matters he tried to add to the money in the king's coffers by blocking some of the outlets through which it flowed away. We have already seen how in 1667 he ordered an investigation intended to uncover spurious claims to noble status. This initiative met with some success, both in reducing the number of noble families and in raising money from others who were forced to pay dearly for the privilege of having their noble status officially recognized.

Similarly, Colbert was able to expand the yield from the ancient royal domain by reclaiming royal lands and rights which had been previously leased, sold or lost in some other way. He also abolished thousands of useless offices which had been created since 1630. The short-term financial advantages accruing to the crown from such creations had been quickly overtaken by the expense of paying the annual salaries. He was equally ruthless towards investors in state funds. Their lump sum deposits were of little help to the government when set against the interest which further drained its limited resources. Colbert abolished half of these annuities and greatly reduced the rate of payment of the remainder.

Besides reducing the losses, Colbert also improved the tax yield in several respects. The clergy were persuaded to increase their annual contribution, the 'free gift', to the exchequer. The assessment of the *taille* was modified so as to increase the rate when the levy was on landowners and to reduce it when it was not, since the landowners were better able to sustain the burden. In the area of indirect taxation, Colbert took steps to rationalize the system of tax-farming, a policy culminating in 1668 with the amalgamation of a range of leases under the heading of the United Farms. By this arrangement a single syndicate took over responsibility for the indirect taxes raised from internal customs dues and from the sale of salt, food and drink. The immediate effect of this re-organization was to improve the tax yield sufficiently to enable Colbert to reduce the *taille*.

All these fiscal measures were introduced between 1661 and 1671, and as a result the king's real income doubled. With the exception of the relatively small-scale War of Devolution (1667–8) these were years of tranquillity for France. However, both the tranquillity and the government's financial health were shattered by the Dutch War (1672–9) and by the deepening international conflicts which followed to the end of the reign. Yet it would be wrong to suggest that Colbert was opposed to war. He understood that war was the routine business of princes. As a devoted servant of Louis XIV he envisaged his own task as being to contribute to the glory of his master's reputation and thereby to his country's security. He was less concerned, therefore, with the question of whether war might come than with the kingdom's state of preparedness when it came. He was no less anxious than the king to embark on the Dutch War.

It is important to appreciate that Colbert's fundamental outlook was not that of a cautious treasury expert anxious to balance the budget, but that of a gifted official totally committed to the king's service. For that reason he was prepared in the 1670s, when the needs of war demanded, to reverse his earlier policies. Useless offices were once again sold, and so were parts of the royal domain. Old taxes were revived and new ones invented. Investors were once more encouraged to lend money to the government with the promise of interest in excess of 7 per cent, in defiance of the 5 per cent legal limit which he himself had pronounced in 1665. He was forced, too, to borrow from tax-farmers at home and from foreign bankers. In 1683, the year of Colbert's death, the effects of the recent conflict still dominated the budget: there was a war debt of nearly 18 million *livres* and an overall deficit of 28 million. This latter figure was equivalent to just under two million pounds sterling, about the amount of England's annual public expenditure at that time. In the light of these figures it is tempting to argue that Colbert's fiscal policies failed. Such a stance, however, would be misleading. For we must judge him according to the priorities which he and his master, the king, accepted as natural, and not according to those of much later generations.

Colbert's overriding concern to promote the mutual reputation of the king and his state illuminates all the other areas of his public life. In line with the western European view which had been dominant since the end of the Middle Ages, Colbert adopted a mercantilist outlook. That meant the belief in a finite amount of wealth in the world which in turn suggested that the power of states depended upon their ability to hold a significant portion of that wealth. Since France possessed no precious metals of her own she would have to acquire gold and silver through the enterprise of her merchants and busisnessmen. This mercantilist view lies at the root of Colbert's hostility to the Dutch. Their merchant fleets dominated the international carrying trade and made it very difficult for French merchants to break into lucrative world markets.

With the fervour of the true bureaucrat, Colbert sought to regulate French economic affairs. He believed that such a policy of close control would help France to overcome her commercial rivals and, more important, would pave the way for that era of Bourbon hegemony which was his ultimate objective. Hence a wide range of industrial enterprises were established under government auspices and control. They included some famous and successful creations, like the Gobelins Tapestry works designated in 1667 as 'Makers of Furniture to the Crown'. However, many other ventures succumbed during the 1670s when the expenses of the Dutch War monopolized the king's financial resources.

In the same mercantilist spirit Colbert founded a number of trading companies. Between 1664 and 1670 the East and West Indies Companies, the Levant Company and the Northern Company were all established. Precisely half way through this period, in 1667, he introduced a prohititive tariff aimed against Dutch and English trading rivals. At the same time he tried to encourage colonial development in Canada and the West Indies. Most important, he worked at the re-establishment of a royal navy.

Possession of a powerful fleet was for Colbert a matter of the greatest significance. In the first place it would help to guarantee the security of the king's realm not only in wartime but also as a constant shield behind which a French mercantile fleet might emerge to challenge the domination of Dutch and English fleets. Second, it would stimulate the emergence of a home-based naval industry which would free France from a dangerous dependence upon the Baltic trade in naval stores which was in Dutch hands. It would also bring wealth to previously impoverished regions of the country, a fact which would assist the king's government in its quest for taxes. With Colbert's enthusiastic backing, therefore, the French royal navy grew from some two dozen craft in 1661 to 140 by 1677. He instituted a new system of naval recruitment and rebuilt the arsenals at Toulon and Rochefort, and the naval hospitals in the various ports. At Brest he established a major port facing England. Finally he established schools of marine engineering, hydrography and cartography which acquired enduring reputations.

Colbert's fundamental concern, to buttress the power and the reputation of Louis XIV and his state, is most clearly demonstrated through his office of superintendent of the king's buildings. He believed that royal palaces and the capital itself should reflect and contribute to the grandeur of the royal régime. Under his aegis Paris acquired splendid new buildings such as the great hospital for discharged soldiers, the Invalides, while Perrault's famous façade was added to the east end of the Louvre palace. Colbert wanted not only architects but artists of every kind to lend their skills to the greater glory of *le roi soleil*. In 1663 he established the *Petite Académie* to assist in this work of harmonization. Paintings, tapestries, inscriptions, operas, poems, statues, all were submitted to the academy's scrutiny so that the king's name could be fittingly honoured. Its supreme achievement was the production of some 300 medals celebrating the reign. The result was art, sometimes of high quality, which was state propaganda at the same time.

Colbert died in 1683. By then, as we have seen, many of his fiscal reforms had been overturned. It was a similar story with regard to many of his industrial projects at home and commercial ventures overseas. The supply of men and material for Canada had dried up by 1673. In the following year the West Indies Company went into liquidation. The East Indies Company survived on a reduced scale but the Northern Company, established to challenge the Dutch in the Baltic, did not outlast the Dutch War. On the credit side, Colbert provided Louis with the economic resources needed to sustain war and a royal navy which provided an additional dimension to French power. That power had made Louis XIV the most feared man in Europe by the time of Colbert's death. In France, too, his awesome image had been masterfully projected by his faithful minister.

It is not satisfactory, however, to sum up Colbert's career in such credit and debit terms. He knew that the king's reputation, which he was so jealous to preserve, depended in part upon success in war, and he knew that warfare was expensive. His policies were therefore designed to ensure that France could sustain her forces in war until victorious. The problem was that there appeared to be no means of maintaining the country's economic buoyancy in the wake of such costly enterprises. Before the end of Louis's reign the establishment of the Bank of England (1694) provided the king's enemies with a solution.

### The Rise of the Phélypeaux

However, such a sophisticated financial mechanism could not be readily adapted to France's political structure. Colbert's successors had to contend as best they could with a fiscal system which, in the face of prolonged war expenditure, lacked resilience. After a modest financial recovery under Colbert's peace-time successor as controller-general, Le Peletier, who was related to the Le Telliers, the old problems reappeared during the Nine Years War (1688–97).

The new controller-general was a member of the Phélypeaux family, the Count de Pontchartrain, who, like Colbert before him, also acquired the office of secretary of state for the marine. When Pontchartrain became chancellor in 1699 his son Jérôme succeeded him in the marine office, though not as controller-general. That post went to Michel Chamillart, a protégé of Louis's wife, Madame de Maintenon. Jérôme Phélypeaux remained in charge of the marine until the king's death. The Pontchartrains, father and son, made commercial expansion an important strategic element in France's international relations. They were successful enough to persuade the king to define the War of the Spanish Succession as a struggle for the commerce of the Spanish Indies and the riches which they produced, though it is doubtful whether Louis really believed that to be so.

The Phélypeaux played a major role in the establishment of the Council of Commerce in 1700. Most historians have viewed the Council's foundation as reflecting the weakness and uncertainty of the king's government in the last years of the reign and the growing demands of the merchant community to control policy, for the Council contained thirteeen deputies from the major cities, who were prominent and experienced traders. It might well appear that these deputies would dictate commercial policy to the six royal commissioners who completed the Council's personnel. However, an American historian, Thomas Schaeper, has recently cast doubt upon this standard interpretation. He points out that the government had been consulting business interests for a century before 1700 and that Pontchartrain's intention in recommending the establishment of a consultative Council of Commerce was to improve the flow of expert advice to the government. This was in accordance with the king's own wishes.

What the Council in fact represented was another stage in the developing bureaucracy of Louis XIV's government. It is incorrect to assume that failures in royal policy during Louis's declining years were due to the absence of strong and effective ministers. The reality was simply that government was becoming too complex, too dependent on officials and experts to allow even the most capable of individuals complete freedom of action. Even the king himself was enmeshed in the spider's web of bureaucracy.

With the outbreak of the War of the Spanish Succession, however, the government was again faced with the problem of how to raise adequate financial resources without the instrument of a sophisticated banking system. Once more it had to turn to short-term expedients: the sale of offices, forced loans from existing office holders, manipulation of the currency, extensive borrowing from financiers and bankers, mortgaging the kingdom's tax revenues in advance, and flooding the country with government bills that took the place of coin and led to massive inflation.

By the time of Louis XIV's death the national debt stood at more than 2,000 million *livres*, with much of the following year's revenue already spent. During the concluding years of the reign (1708–15) the commission of controller-general of finance was again held by a member of the Colbert family. Nicholas Desmaretz, who was a nephew of the great minister, introduced a deflationary régime in a desperate attempt to restore the country's financial equilibrium. The result was stagnation in commerce and agriculture as people chose to hoard their money rather than risk losing it. The ground was thus prepared for John Law's radical attempt to restore the economy in the following reign, by encouraging the constant circulation of money through the agency of a state bank.

24

Michel le Tellier was a member of that influential trio of ministers, along with Colbert and Lionne, who dominated the High Council at the beginning of the king's personal reign. He was secretary of state for war until his resignation in 1677 in favour of his son, the Marquis de Louvois. The two men were together responsible for transforming the French army into the most powerful and cohesive force in Europe, thereby enabling Louis to gratify his thirst for *gloire* in the field of foreign affairs.

The transformation of the French army by Le Tellier and Louvois provides another example of the way in which the individual's freedom of action in the French state was becoming subordinate to ideas of bureaucratic organization. It was important, for example, to instil into the officer corps the notion of service to the king's cause, the quality of which would depend upon ability rather than upon family background. The tradition of noble ownership of regiments had to be broken. Consequently, the new officers were to be trained as professionals able to take orders from social inferiors as well as to give them. Though the officer class remained largely noble, men of talent were enabled to rise from relatively humble origins to high military office. One of Louis XIV's greatest soldiers, the Marquis de Vauban, came from a poor gentry family. The recruitment of the troops was made the responsibility of the intendants. Their tasks included organizing military supplies and accommodation. They were also in charge of military discipline. War commissioners were appointed at a local level to liaise with the intendants, and intendants and commissioners reported directly and regularly to the secretary of state for war. In addition, the latter sent inspectors from time to time to check on the effectiveness of the local operation.

Thus the French army ceased to be a loose confederation of units raised by great noblemen and hired out to the crown. Instead it became a formidable state machine numbering some 350,000 men by the end of Louis XIV's reign. Most of these troops were Frenchmen and volunteers. Indeed, intendants forbade the practice of recruitment by force. However, Louvois did introduce a conscript militia in 1688 to bolster the army for the duration of the Nine Years War which was just beginning. Recruitment which was by lot at parish level was intended to produce some 25,000 additional troops, though that number grew when the militia was re-introduced during the War of the Spanish Succession.

The military reforms of Le Tellier and his son Louvois brought into being a new kind of royal army, centrally directed and controlled, whose soldiers all wore the king's uniform. Yet paradoxically the commander-in-chief, Louis XIV himself, did not choose to lead his soldiers into battle as most of his predecessors had done. He contented himself with near ceremonial appearances at sieges. This was not because the king was a physical coward: there is no evidence to that effect. Rather it was because he recognized that warfare had become a complex business best left to professional soldiers. Far from being diminished by that fact, the authority at his command was greatly strengthened.

## RELIGIOUS ISSUES

### The Huguenots and the Revocation of the Edict of Nantes

Michel Le Tellier and his son Louvois were both influential in bringing about one of the most controversial episodes of the reign, the decision to stamp out French Protestantism by revoking the law which had given it protection since 1598.

The Edict of Nantes had healed the deep wounds caused by the Wars of Religion in France (1562–98) by recognizing the Huguenots' right to practise their faith without the risk of persecution. However, persecution did recommence in the early years of Louis XIV's direct rule. The king's preference was to rule over a realm united by faith as well as by loyalty to the ruler. His conventional view of the role of religion in the state harked back to the principle of *cuius regio eius religio*, developed after the religious map of Europe had been redrawn as a result of the coming of the Reformation. Then it was accepted that the subjects' religion must conform to that of the ruler.

There was never any doubt in Louis's mind that his state would be more secure if all the subjects shared the Catholicism of the Most Christian King. Besides, there was an implied affront to his *gloire*, to the family honour, in the existence of this well-entrenched minority, despite the fact that they had remained entirely loyal to the king, even during the civil war of the *Frondes*. There is little doubt, therefore, that Louis wished to make the Huguenots conform; the more interesting question is why he chose to act when he did.

A number of factors came together to account for the train of events. There is evidence from the late 1670s that under the influence of Madame de Maintenon the king was beginning to regret the excesses of his youth and was becoming conscience-stricken at his failure to convert the heretics among his subjects. At the same time the Dutch War came to an end with the Peace of Nijmwegen (1678–9), a settlement acknowledging Louis's domination of Western Europe and freeing him to put his own kingdom in order.

Finally, towards the close of the 1670s Colbert's influence began to diminish as that of the minister of war, Louvois, grew. Colbert, whose economic policies included encouraging Protestants to settle in France, opposed persecution of the Huguenots. Louvois on the contrary favoured a brutal policy of enforced conversion, spear-headed by the infamous dragonnades, royal troops who were quartered on Protestant families and allowed to terrorize them into renouncing their faith. After 1679, therefore, the tempo of official persecution quickened, and the provisions of the Edict of Nantes were increasingly flouted and circumvented.

During the first half of the 1680s several additional factors added to the pressure which culminated in 1685 with the Edict of Fontainebleau, revoking the Edict of Nantes. During these years the king's relations with the Pope, Innocent XI, reached a particularly low level for two reasons. Louis had been in dispute with the Papacy since 1675 over his attempt to extend the traditional right of *régale*, which allowed the king to administer vacant bishoprics in France and draw revenue from them. The argument came to a head in 1682 with the publication of the Gallican Articles as a law of the French state. These articles restated the French or Gallican Church's tradition of independence within the Catholic fold, in particular restricting papal authority over the king and the bishops. Then, in the following year, Louis refused a plea to join a crusade against the Ottoman Turks, whose forces were besieging Vienna. The city was relieved by the Imperial armies and Louis's rival, the Habsburg Emperor Leopold I, was acclaimed as the champion of Christendom. His Most Christian Majesty, on the other hand, remained at odds with the Pope and appeared to be putting considerations of political expediency before his obligation to defend the faith. Louis, therefore, was anxious to demonstrate his orthodoxy and the pressure to do so became even more intense after February 1685 when the zealous Catholic James II became King of England. Encouraged by the dying Le Tellier, now chancellor of France, Louis signed the Edict of Fontainebleau in October 1685.

Henceforth the practice of the Protestant religion was proscribed and harsh measures were employed to enforce the edict, including the introduction of the death penalty for those who defied it. About 200,000 people, some 10 per cent of the Huguenot population, which was itself 10 per cent of the total population of France, left the country in the decades following 1685. Though forbidden to emigrate, many Huguenot lay people fled the country, while their ministers were banished. Those who remained either continued to practise their religion in secret or accepted conversion with a marked lack of enthusiasm. However, seventeen years after the revocation of the Edict of Nantes, a Protestant rebellion, the revolt of the Camisards, broke out in the mountains of the Cevennes in south-eastern France (1702–5). It proved serious enough to persuade the king to send one of his most distinguished soldiers, Marshal Villars, to the region. By astutely combining force with clemency the Marshal was able to suppress the insurrection. But one consequence of the revolt was to restore some vigour to French Protestantism, although it remained officially banned until 1787, when the movement regained legal recognition.

It was long believed by historians that the emigration had serious effects upon France's economy, in particular upon domestic industries like the manufacture of silk and woollen fabrics, and upon overseas trade where Huguenot industrialists and shippers were well established. However, that view has now been modified. Warren C. Scoville has soundly argued that although there can be no doubting France's loss of much technical and entrepreneurial expertise to the rest of Europe, the last two wars of Louis XIV's reign offer a better explanation for French economic stagnation in the years after 1685.

In another sense, however, Louis did increase France's vulnerability in Europe as a result of his revocation. Henceforth he was perceived by his rivals as a threat to European security. It therefore proved easier for his arch-enemy, William of Orange, to organize powerful coalitions against him.

One final question should be asked about the whole episode of the revocation. What was Louis XIV's own responsibility? There is some evidence to suggest that the king did not fully appreciate nor approve of the draconian methods involved in the drive for conversion up to 1685. Louis was not personally a cruel man as some of those who served him certainly were, but he wanted the Huguenot problem solved and it is fair to assume that he allowed the brutal realities, which of course he did not witness at first hand, to fade before that central objective. He may even have allowed himself to be persuaded by 1685, quite incorrectly, that the Edict of Nantes no longer served any purpose since only a handful of Huguenots continued to resist conversion.

## Jansenism

The Catholic doctrine of Jansenism originated in the *Augustinus* (1640) of Cornelius Jansen, Bishop of Ypres. As the title of his work suggests, Bishop Jansen was much influenced by the pessimistic writings of Saint Augustine. Consequently, he stressed man's inability to achieve salvation except through the acquisition of divine grace, which he believed was only bestowed upon a few.

His teaching was taken up by some within the French Church and its adherents formed a close-knit and defiant group. Even the theologians found it difficult to define precisely what this group believed, so the king – who was no theologian – had very little idea at all. Nevertheless, throughout his reign he remained hostile to the Jansenists. His chief reason, which applied also to the Huguenots, was simply the fact that they did not conform. They therefore represented a divisive, unreliable element among his subjects, an affront to royal dignity and authority. Indeed, there was evidence to link some Jansenists with the *Frondes*: this distinguished them from the Huguenots, who remained loyal throughout the civil wars.

Louis also distrusted the movement because of its democratic spirit. It emphasized the role of ordinary priests in the government of the Church, and of laymen in the conduct of church services. The spread of such ideas would threaten to undermine the authoritarian, strictly regulated hierarchy of Church and State over which Louis presided. A third reason for the king's dislike of Jansenism lay in its evident disapproval of worldly luxury and display, and in the different values it represented. The movement implicitly criticized all that Versailles represented, that aura of regal magnificence in which the Sun-king gloried.

What most concerned Louis, however, was the fact that Jansenism possessed its own headquarters at the convent of Port-Royal-des-Champs, just south of Versailles. Inspired by the *abbé* de Saint Cyran and by the Arnauld family, Port-Royal posed a challenge to both the spiritual and secular establishments. From this Jansenist centre was disseminated not only the doctrine of individual worth, founded on simplicity and personal contemplation, but also a series of doctrinal and devotional texts. Conversely, Port-Royal drew within its walls a number of distinguished writers, including two of the giant intellects of

29

the seventeenth century, the mathematician and philosopher, Blaise Pascal, and the poet, Jean Racine.

Its most influential theologian was Antoine Arnauld, who was involved in conflict with the Papacy during the 1650s. In 1653 the Pope condemned as heretical five propositions attributed to the writing of Bishop Jansen. Arnauld accepted that these propositions were worthy of condemnation but maintained that they were not to be found in the *Augustinus*. The Pope tried again in 1656, only to be met with the same tactic.

Several years later, when Louis reached his majority, he at once revealed his hostility towards the recalcitrant convent. By a royal council decree of 1661, many of the residents of Port-Royal were expelled, their leaders, including Arnauld, fled, and the schools attached to the convent were closed down. But some of the French bishops were more cautious than the king. They expressed concern that certain papal pronouncements relating to the Jansenist controversy could not be reconciled with Gallican doctrine. Their reservations anticipated the coming battle between the French king and the Papacy over the Gallican Liberties. Eventually a truce was arranged, the so-called Peace of the Church of 1668. The community of Port-Royal was fully restored to the Catholic fold, and Pope, king and bishops accepted a compromise, a form of words negotiated by Lionne which papered over the theological cracks.

However, Louis's attitude to the convent still continued to be hostile for the reasons stated above. In 1679, shortly after the signing of the Peace of Nijmwegen, the king forbade both confessors and novices to remain at Port-Royal. This policy was intended to lead gradually to the convent's spiritual decline. But meanwhile Louis had become embroiled in the protracted argument with Pope Innocent XI over the liberties of the Gallican Church. While it continued, the issue of Jansenism remained a secondary consideration. It was only in 1693, when France's security in Europe was coming under threat, that Louis made a grudging peace with the Papacy by suspending, though not revoking, the Gallican Articles of 1682.

The way was then clear for a renewed attack on Jansenism and the opportunity was provided by the appearance in 1692 of a book by a Jansenist priest, Pasquier Quesnel, entitled *Moral Reflections on the New Testament*. Louis now looked to Rome for a definitive condemnation of Jansenist doctrine. At the same time he insisted that any papal pronouncement should conform with the principles enunciated by the Gallican Articles.

Nevertheless, the papal bull *Vineam Domini*, published in 1705, failed to resolve the conflict since the community of Port-Royal refused to accept it without certain qualifications. Eventually the king decided on drastic action. A council decree of October 1709 ordered the community to be dispersed. The deserted convent then became a place of Jansenist pilgrimage so that in 1711 the king ordered its complete destruction. This brutal assault shocked some people in France just as, on a more significant scale, Louis's treatment of the Huguenots had earlier affected opinion in Europe. As with the Huguenots, there is evidence that royal hostility to Jansenism was political rather than personal. While remaining uncompromising in his determination to destroy what he perceived to be a dangerous opposition group within the state, Louis maintained friendly relations with the great Racine, an honoured guest at Versailles. Furthermore, in accordance with his own wishes, Racine was buried at Port-Royal in 1699. We also know that amongst friends Louis could be persuaded to speak approvingly of the community's reputation for sanctity.

In the closing years of his reign the old king became increasingly anxious to leave a kingdom united in doctrinal purity in order to facilitate his own eternal salvation. He was impatient with the Gallican restrictions which he had so stoutly defended thirty years earlier. He requested the Pope, Clement XI, to issue a once-and-for-all condemnation of Jansenism in the form of a papal pronouncement which he promised the Pope he would enforce in France. The result was the bull *Unigenitus* (1713).

However, religious peace did not ensue. Gallicans in the *Parlement* of Paris, in the faculty of Theology of the Sorbonne, and among the French bishops united against the bull and against the king's authoritarian methods, which ignored Gallican tradition. The dispute had not been settled by the time of Louis's death in 1715. It would continue to disturb the peace of Church and State far down into the eighteenth century.

Because religion and politics were inextricably united in his age, Louis XIV was understandably as anxious to prevent theological division in his state as civil disturbance. That his religious policy was on the whole unsuccessful may be partly accounted for by political miscalculation on his part and by the insensitivity of his approach. But there was also a contradiction at the heart of his policy. The king's efforts to build a powerful centralized state, which depended upon the creation of a secular ethos, was hindered so long as politics remained tied to its religious moorings. In addition, his determination to overcome Jansenism eventually led Louis to reverse his Gallican policy of support for the national Church. Instead, he came to depend upon an outside power, the Papacy, to make his policies effective, thereby undermining his own authority at home.

## Foreign policy

### INTRODUCTION

Louis XIV's chief preoccupation was foreign policy: the regulation of the complex relationship between France and other European states. Ever since the beginning of modern international diplomacy in fifteenth-century Italy, princes had given priority to maintaining their power at their neighbours' expense. Because for the most part they represented family dynasties, the rulers of states, including Louis XIV, tended to view international agreements as they viewed private legal contracts. Contemporaries saw nothing odd in the fact that a major international settlement like the Treaty of the Pyrenees (1659), which ended the Thirty Years' War between France and Spain, should also contain arrangements for Louis XIV's marriage to a Spanish princess, Maria Theresa, as well as provisions for the restoration of the French estates of the rebel Prince de Condé.

However, in the course of Louis XIV's long reign other considerations began to loom large: what were the rights of the state as opposed to those of the ruling family and what rights had the subjects in the painful and expensive business of waging war? We have already seen how in religious affairs Louis's objectives were frustrated by conflicting ideas. Similarly, in the conduct of his foreign policy the king was an inevitable victim of changing attitudes and circumstances.

He was assisted in the implementation of his foreign policy by a number of distinguished secretaries of state, Lionne, Arnauld de Pomponne, Colbert de Croissy, brother of the great Colbert, and Croissy's son, the Marquis de Torcy, who further united these governing families by marrying the daughter of Pomponne. Yet none of them ran foreign affairs: that was pre-eminently the king's business, even at the end of the reign when the developing bureaucratic organization gave Torcy greater knowledge and expertise than any of his predecessors had possessed. Torcy could take the initiative more regularly, but not the final decisions.

Louis's chief concern was to maintain the security of his state. Throughout Europe governments shared that view of the primacy of security so that foreign policy was universally perceived as a never-ending series of adjustments, by means of diplomacy or war, to the rights and territories of states. That is still the situation today. However, Louis XIV's government had no national ideology with which to justify its actions. Instead, it depended upon that concept of family honour and reputation which bound the king to aim for a glorious inheritance for his successors. There was a thin dividing line, as there still is, between the defensive needs of a régime threatened by powerful neighbours and the offensive posture of a state determined to establish its security on the soundest footing. Louis responded to both pressures in the course of his reign.

### THE WAR OF DEVOLUTION (1667–8)

Behind many of Louis XIV's foreign policy initiatives lay the problem of the Spanish Succession. In 1665 Charles II succeeded as King of Spain and heir to the great Spanish Empire in Europe and overseas. Spain had been in decline for much of the century but she still possessed extensive lands in Europe, including Milan, Naples and Sicily, as well as Franche-Comté and the Spanish Netherlands on France's eastern and north-eastern frontiers. The Spanish Habsburgs traditionally allied with the family's German branch, headed by the Emperor. Like his predecessors, Louis XIV was well aware that France was surrounded by a potentially threatening power-bloc. The boy-king, Charles II, was an invalid who was not expected to live long and was thought most unlikely to produce an heir. In that situation Louis's thoughts were bound to turn to the question of the Spanish inheritance. They did so regularly during his reign, though it would be an overstatement to suggest that he planned his foreign policy with that issue constantly in mind.

Following the accession of Charles II, Louis decided to invade the Spanish Netherlands, justifying his action in characteristic dynastic fashion. His lawyers pointed out that according to the law of succession in Brabant, which was part of the Spanish Netherlands, the daughter of a first marriage retained her rights even when a son was born to her father by a second marriage. Louis then applied this argument to the case of his wife, Maria Theresa, who was the elder half-sister of the new king of Spain.

In the war that followed, Louis's diplomacy, allied with superior military strength, enabled him to make several significant gains. He resisted the temptation to press his military superiority to the point of provoking a coalition against him. At the Treaty of Aix-la-Chapelle (1668) France acquired a number of key fortresses, including Tournai and Charleroi, situated well within the frontier of the Spanish Netherlands. It was a temporary settlement but at least it strengthened France's ability to protect Paris, which lay so close to this vulnerable frontier.

One other benefit accrued to Louis from this war. Aided by his chief adviser on foreign affairs, Hugues de Lionne, who had earlier distinguished himself in negotiations including those leading to the Treaty of the Pyrenees, Louis succeeded in persuading the Emperor to agree to a partition of the Spanish Empire in the event of the death of Charles II without heirs. The long-term significance of this agreement was that the Emperor, who was himself a strong candidate for the succession, appeared to accept that the Bourbons too retained a justifiable claim to the Spanish throne. That was certainly Louis's interpretation and it provided a precedent for two further partition treaties later in the reign.

### THE DUTCH WAR (1672–8/9)

In his Memoirs for the year 1668 Louis made it perfectly clear that he had chosen to play down his ambitions for the moment in order to make further gains later. The Dutch War, planned from the moment the War of Devolution ended, was intended to complete the victory only partially secured at Aix-la-Chapelle. The Dutch were the natural enemy. Louis disliked their republicanism, their Calvinist religion and their trading ethos, all of which contrasted sharply with the principles of divine-right monarchy in France. But there was also a sound strategic reason why the Dutch had to be defeated: France's efforts to strengthen her weak north-eastern frontier would inevitably provoke a hostile response from the Dutch Republic, fearful of French domination of the Spanish Netherlands. Already during the War of Devolution mediation by a Triple Alliance, consisting of the Dutch Republic, England and Sweden, had helped to persuade Louis to embrace a policy of moderation. He totally abandoned that policy during the Dutch War.

34

In 1672 the French armies crossed the Rhine via the imperial bishopric of Liège and entered the Dutch Republic. They carried all before them and the Dutch States-General promptly sued for peace. Louis's terms amounted to a demand for unconditional surrender, and the opportunity for peace passed. The Dutch had already flooded the country. William, Prince of Orange, the stadholder of the richest province, Holland, proceeded to organize the opposition. Other European powers prepared to unite against the French threat, shocked by the brutal policies inspired by the minister of war, Louvois, who had replaced Lionne's moderate successor, Pomponne. In 1673 the Dutch were joined by Spain, the Emperor, Brandenburg and Lorraine in the kind of anti-French coalition which Louis had earlier taken great pains to avert. A year later British public opinion forced the Stuart king, Charles II, to withdraw from the war which he had entered on the French side in accordance with the terms of the Secret Treaty of Dover (1670).

The war continued for another four years during which the French made significant gains against Spain, including the annexation of the province of Franche-Comté on France's eastern frontier (1674). However, the Dutch maintained their resistance to such good effect that in the peace settlement signed at Nijmwegen in 1678 France returned the important fortress of Maastricht which protected the entry to the Dutch Republic and agreed to rescind Colbert's harsh tariff laws of 1667. On the other hand, Louis acquired from Spain Franche-Comté and a number of key fortresses on the frontier between France and the Spanish Netherlands, including Condé, Valenciennes, Ypres and Saint-Omer. The Congress of Nijmwegen concluded with an agreement with the Emperor signed in February 1679, whereby Louis retained the strategic city of Freiburg east of the Rhine which helped to protect French possessions in Alsace.

The Peace of Nijmwegen was for Louis XIV a successful outcome of the Dutch War, though not the triumph which he envisaged when it began. He learned that the Spanish Netherlands could not be overrun against Dutch wishes and that a war prosecuted with such lack of moderation was likely to provoke the most stubborn opposition from his enemies. It also made them more determined to resist the king later when his ambitions seemed to threaten Europe, though, as we shall see, their own lack of moderation in this regard ironically may have helped Louis to escape the worst consequences of defeat in the War of the Spanish Succession. The king also learned to concentrate on less spectacular policies to ensure his kingdom's security.

This is a suitable point at which to take up the argument most notably expounded by Ragnhild Hatton. She contends that a determined defensive strategy was an important element of Louis XIV's foreign policy, though it was obscured by his aggressive attitude towards the Dutch. We have already noted how the French capital, Paris, was vulnerable to attack from the Spanish Netherlands. There were other entrances to the kingdom, too, which the king had been anxious to close to his enemies. One, the port of Dunkirk, he succeeded in closing in 1662 when he bought it from Charles II, the king of England. The threat from the Southern Netherlands was removed after 1678; Louis's great military engineer, Vauban, built a system of fortresses linked by water behind the new, straightened frontier agreed at the Peace of Nijmwegen. This so-called iron barrier proved its worth during the War of the Spanish Succession. France's weakness on the eastern frontier was eased by the acquisition of Franche-Comté in the same settlement, but the situation in that region remained confused and potentially dangerous.

There were still a number of gateways from the Empire through which enemies of France might threaten the state's security. The three imperial bishoprics of Metz, Toul and Verdun were strategically situated on the north-eastern frontier. They had been occupied by French troops since 1552 but it was only at the Peace of Westphalia (1648) that they were finally acknowledged as sovereign possessions of the French king. Furthermore, the Emperor continued throughout Louis's reign to work for their reversal to imperial status. South of the bishoprics lay the duchy of Lorraine. Louis did not succeed in his cherished ambition to incorporate this duchy into his kingdom, although it was occupied by French troops for long periods. It remained part of the Empire and as such a half-open door into France. East of Lorraine lay Alsace and the free city of Strasbourg, the key to the Rhine and the upper Danube. At the Peace of Westphalia French rights in Alsace had been stated in a very ambiguous fashion, particularly in respect to its ten towns, the so-called Decapole (which did not include Strasbourg). Here, then, was another insecure frontier region, a fact of which Louis was made particularly aware during the Dutch War, when Imperial armies entered Alsace by way of Strasbourg.

It is against this background that we should study Louis's policy of *réunions*. This was an attempt, characteristic of dynastic methods, to employ legal arguments to extend the king's authority over areas of disputed and uncertain sovereignty. The king's chief judicial courts in the regions of Franche-Comté, Alsace, Lorraine, Metz, Toul and Verdun were commanded to determine what additional territories were dependent upon those already properly acquired by Louis at Westphalia and Nijmwegen. Not surprisingly the additions proved to be extensive and strategically important. They could not, however, be stretched to include Strasbourg itself, despite the fact that the city was one of the vital bulwarks in any effective defence of the eastern frontier. To the policy of legalistic opportunism, therefore, Louis added the weight of military force. Strasbourg was occupied by French troops in September 1681.

This was a grievous blow to the Emperor since the possession of Strasbourg opened the way for French armies to march towards the Danube and Vienna. In fairness to Louis, however, it was equally true that Strasbourg under imperial control left France dangerously exposed to invasion. In any case there was little the Emperor could do about it since he was now fully committed to the defence of Vienna against the Turks. That fact encouraged Louis to continue to back his *réunion* strategy with military sorties into the Spanish Netherlands. Eventually Spain was provoked into declaring war (1683), hopeful that the lifting of the siege of Vienna a month earlier would free the Emperor to join an anti-French coalition. That hope proved illusory. French troops captured the Spanish fortress of Luxembourg, one of the main objectives of the *réunion* policy, and this success forced both Spain and the Emperor to agree to the Truce of Ratisbon (1684).

Ratisbon marked a high point among Louis XIV's foreign policy achievements. The Emperor, the princes of the Empire, and Spain signed a twenty-year truce accepting for that period France's continued occupation of Lorraine, her acquisition of Strasbourg and the *réunion* lands including Luxembourg. It appeared that the vulnerable eastern and north-eastern frontiers had been firmly secured.

The defensive needs of the kingdom therefore were a major pre-occupation behind Louis XIV's foreign policy and we shall return to them later. Yet the aggressive and opportunistic implementation of Louis's policy understandably persuaded those threatened by it that the king's intention was expansionist and his ambitions unlimited. There had been acts of gratuitous violence too, which underlined the arrogance and ruthlessness of French conduct: the scorched earth policy during the Dutch War and the destruction by naval barrage of the free city of Genoa (1684) for having the effrontery to assist Spain. Louis subsequently refused to make peace with the city until its civic leaders had visited Versailles to demonstrate their abject submission before the Sunking. Louis himself must bear the responsibility for such actions, though he was following the promptings of his secretaries of state for war and the navy, Louvois and Colbert's son, the Marquis de Seignelay, who succeeded his father in 1683. The Revocation of the Edict of Nantes in the year after Ratisbon, with its accompanying brutality, reinforced the belief of Louis's enemies that the king's ambitions threatened them all. The prospect of a united front against France began to loom.

### THE NINE YEARS WAR (1688–97)

Despite his triumph at Ratisbon, the French king did not feel entirely secure. He knew that the Emperor was intent on redressing the balance in the west once he had overcome the threat from the Ottoman Empire in the east. Leopold began to enjoy a series of victories over the Turks so that by 1687 most of Hungary was in Habsburg hands. The Imperial armies were by this time a formidable force and the Emperor's power and prestige were persuading lesser German princes, like the rulers of Bavaria and Brandenburg, to move out of Louis XIV's orbit and into Leopold's.

In addition, Louis could not ignore the formidable William of Orange, now harbouring the ambition to become king of England, who posed a threat much closer to home. Consequently, Louis's concern with the security of his eastern frontier once more became acute. His defensive strategy was now extended to two Rhineland objectives beyond his boundaries, the electorate of Cologne and the fortress of Phillipsburg on the right bank of the river beyond the Palatinate. Control of Cologne would provide a barrier in northern Germany and a base from which to threaten the Dutch Republic.

When the archbishop-elector died in June 1688, the French king therefore was determined that his favoured candidate, Cardinal Fürstenberg, the bishop of Strasbourg, should become the new spiritual ruler of the electorate of Cologne. However, his hopes were dashed by Innocent XI with whom Louis was still on bad terms. The Pope conferred the archbishopric upon Fürstenberg's rival, a brother of the Elector of Bavaria, who enjoyed the support of William of Orange and the Emperor Leopold.

In September 1688 French troops marched into Cologne and across the Palatinate to Phillipsburg. As in the War of Devolution, Louis appealed to the right of family inheritance to justify his invasion of the Palatinate. For his sister-in-law was herself a sister of the late Elector Palatine with a possible claim to part of her brother's electorate. The true reason, however, was the king's growing conviction that Alsace in particular would be vulnerable to imperial assault when the expected defeat of the Turks was accomplished. Although the French forces met with some success, Phillipsburg falling at the end of October 1688, it soon became clear that the resistance of the German princes would not be easily overcome. Yet the greatest blow to Louis's hopes was struck far away from the Rhineland. In November William of Orange invaded England, drove out Louis's ally, James II, and succeeded him as king. The European balance of power thus moved decisively against France.

Louis's reaction, defensible in terms of the *Realpolitik* of state security, deeply shocked contemporary opinion which had not yet accepted the idea of total war. He withdrew his troops to less exposed positions, ordering them to destroy the towns and ravage the country-side as they retreated, so that an invading army would lack bases and supplies. His devastation of the Palatinate merely tightened the noose by pulling his enemies closer together. They believed that the time had finally come to put an end by joint action to Louis's policy of piecemeal aggression. The Grand Alliance of Vienna was formed between the Emperor, many of the German princes including Brandenburg and Bavaria, England, the Dutch Republic, Spain and Savoy.

The Nine Years' War developed into a military stalemate, though French victories outnumbered those of the Allies. Louis realized that peace could only be achieved through compromise. Yet his willingness to accept terms, and to forego the chance of exploiting the modest military and naval successes won by French arms at Fleurus (1690), Beachy Head (1690), Steenkirk (1692) and Marseille (1693), suggested a fundamental shift in French policy. That may be accounted for by the king's appreciation of the changed military situation; and by the effect that the war was having upon the country's population and economy, both ravaged by three successive bad harvests from 1691 and by the savage winter of 1693–4.

There was another reason for Louis's flexibility, however, and that was the fact that the long-standing problem of the Spanish Succession was reaching a decisive stage. To the surprise of all Europe, Charles II of Spain had survived into the 1690s. Yet his death could not be long delayed and it was now certain that he would have no children to succeed him. The original partition treaty signed by Louis and Leopold in 1668 had been repudiated by the Emperor during the Dutch War. Whenever Charles II died, therefore, a highly volatile state of affairs would exist as Bourbon and Habsburg each claimed the right to succeed to Charles's vast Empire.

Louis had attempted to negotiate secretly with the Emperor during the Nine Years' War. He had offered to renounce all Bourbon claims to the Spanish Succession, provided that the Emperor recognized Louis's sovereignty over the eastern frontier of France, which would be further strengthened by the permanent annexation of Lorraine. He also required that the Austrian and Spanish Habsburg lands should not be united under a single ruler as they had once been under Emperor Charles V (1519–55). The offer provides a measure of Louis's depth of concern for his security in the east. Its rejection made him realize that if such a tempting prize could not buy off the Emperor, he must make other plans to protect his frontier, and at the same time re-assert his family's claim to the Spanish inheritance. Spain had been firmly in the anti-French camp for some time. Charles II's wife, Maria Anna of Neuburg, was a sister-in-law of the Emperor and there was strong support in Madrid for a Habsburg succession. Louis would have been powerless to prevent it if Charles had died whilst the war was still raging. Hence he decided to accept the terms of the Treaty of Ryswick (1697), which enabled him to present a more moderate image, especially to Madrid.

At Ryswick Louis XIV agreed to withdraw from Lorraine and to return to Spain most of the fortresses acquired by means of his *réunion* policy, including Luxembourg. He returned his outposts beyond the Rhine, notably Freiburg and Phillipsburg, to the Empire and recognized William III as King of England despite the fact that his predecessor, James II (whom Louis firmly believed to be still the legitimate king), was living in exile in France. In return the French king was assured of his possession of Strasbourg and Alsace. The vulnerable eastern frontier looked less secure than after Ratisbon, but with Metz, Toul, Verdun, Franche-Comté and Strasbourg, it was a good deal stronger than it had been before the Peace of Westphalia (1648). Besides, Louis now had the opportunity to strengthen his position further as the struggle over the Spanish Succession loomed.

There is another clause in the Treaty of Ryswick which is of particular significance. The Dutch acquired the right to garrison certain fortresses on the border between the Spanish Netherlands and France.

This so-called barrier was intended to delay an invading army from France long enough to allow the Dutch Republic to organize its defences. The concept of national security was beginning to acquire international recognition.

When Louis XIV approached William III in 1698 with the suggestion that they should negotiate a division of the Spanish inheritance between the various claimants, he was extending still further the idea of security as the basis of international agreements. The fact was that William himself had no claim to the Spanish Empire. But he was the King of England and stadholder in the Dutch Republic, which made him the effective leader of the most powerful maritime states in Western Europe. He was thus in a strong position to influence any European settlement; and to exert pressure on his old ally, the Emperor, in Vienna. His involvement in the Partition Treaties of 1698 and 1700 demonstrates therefore how spectacularly the idea of collective security was beginning to challenge traditional principles of dynastic inheritance even in the mind of an arch-dynast like Louis XIV.

The First Partition Treaty allocated Spain itself, the Spanish Netherlands and the overseas Empire to the electoral Prince of Bavaria, Joseph Ferdinand. This young child derived his claim from his mother, a daughter of the Emperor Leopold. Leopold's second son, the Archduke Charles, was to receive the duchy of Milan in northern Italy, and Louis XIV's heir, the Dauphin, would acquire Naples and Sicily as well as the Basque province of Guipúzcoa, which was intended to secure France's southern frontier with Spain. However, the electoral Prince of Bavaria died in 1699, necessitating the signing of a Second Partition Treaty in 1700.

By its terms Archduke Charles received Spain, the Spanish Netherlands and the overseas Empire, whilst the Dauphin acquired Milan as well as Naples, Sicily and Guipúzcoa. A Habsburg presence in the Spanish Netherlands was unwelcome to Louis though the treaty stipulated that the Archduke's portion could not be held by the Emperor or his heir, the King of the Romans. However, he had also taken measures in the Second Partition Treaty to ensure that the Spanish and Austrian Habsburgs could not act easily in unison against him. The acquisition of most of the Italian lands by France would have provided a formidable barrier to Habsburg co-operation. Even so, Louis did not envisage a permanent French presence in Italy. He preferred to exchange the Italian lands – Milan for the Duchy of Lorraine and Naples and Sicily for the Duchy of Savoy and Piedmont – in order to reinforce the security of his whole eastern frontier, leaving the Italian peninsula divided between weak rulers. The exchange for Lorraine was actually mooted in the treaty, while discussion between William and Louis over the transference of Savoy and Naples and Sicily were only aborted by the King of Spain's death. These powerful rulers were expounding the radical notion of collective security to the point of requiring the wholesale re-allocation of states. In addition, each treaty envisaged armed intervention by the signatories – the kingdoms of France and England and the United Provinces of the Dutch Republic – against any power which flouted its terms.

Amidst this diplomatic activity, Charles II decided to make a will, leaving the whole Spanish inheritance to Louis XIV's second grandson, Philippe, Duke of Anjou. Then, at last, on 1 November 1700 he died. A few days later Louis accepted the will's validity and rejected the Second Partition Treaty which he had concluded with William III only seven months earlier, in March 1700.

### THE WAR OF THE SPANISH SUCCESSION (1701–13/14)

Louis's decision to accept the will was not easily taken. The treaty offered the prospect of strategic gains for the French state, whereas the will ruled against any union of the two crowns. A Bourbon ruling in Madrid would quickly become a Spaniard in terms of his country's interests, which might not always coincide with those of his French cousins. Yet there were strong pressures pushing Louis towards acceptance. The most immediate was the testament itself which named the Archduke Charles as heir to the Spanish Empire if France chose rejection. The king had no doubt that Leopold would seize his chance to acquire the Spanish Habsburg Empire for the Austrian Habsburgs if he were given the opportunity. Louis was also aware that William III was unlikely to take up arms against his old ally, the Emperor, in defence of the Partition Treaty. There was a final reason, too, which helped to sway the king and that was his attachment to dynasticism.

We have emphasized Louis's concern for security. But it should not be assumed that in clothing this in the legal conventions of family claims and charters Louis was acting hypocritically. He was committed by upbringing and conviction to the belief that legal rights should justify political action. When the opportunity was presented unequivocally to embrace such a view the king was tempted. He did believe in the justice of his family's claim to the Spanish Succession and he was too proud a dynast to turn his back on such a clarion call to glory.

And yet Louis's acceptance of the will did not in itself make war inevitable, except with the Emperor. But in the months following his acceptance he was responsible for a series of actions which were at best indiscreet, at worst provocative. Their cumulative effect was to revive the Grand Alliance and draw France into a disastrous war which came close to destroying all Louis's previous triumphs in foreign policy.

It is difficult to determine why he acted in this fashion. He was well aware of the military threat posed by the Grand Alliance. The Nine Years' War had demonstrated France's new vulnerability, and his actions after Ryswick had been aimed at preventing war, not preparing for it. Two of his provocations may be explained in terms of that profound belief in divine-right kingship which had been vindicated by the contents of Charles II's will. Shortly after his recognition of Philip V as King of Spain, Louis formally proclaimed that his grandson's right to the French Succession remained valid and beyond the power of men to challenge. There are good reasons for believing that Louis did *not* envisage an eventual union of the two crowns, but rather the succession of a junior branch of the Bourbon family, the Orléans, in Spain if Philip should inherit the French throne. But, intoxicated with the justice – as he perceived it – of his grandson's cause, the king failed to say so. The second gesture of this kind occurred in September 1701 when, following the death of the exiled James II, Louis recognized his son as James III, King of England. Again there is evidence that Louis's concern was with the recognition of a principle rather than with a practical assault upon the authority of William III, though by that time he may well have been convinced that a major war was inevitable.

An earlier provocative act, in February 1701, had been the decision to send French troops to take over the Dutch barrier fortresses in the Southern Netherlands. Since at that time the Dutch Republic had not yet recognized Philip V as sovereign in the Spanish Netherlands and since Louis was acting with his grandson's approval, an argument could be made in Louis's defence. But the move simply added to the deep suspicion of the king's motives which his enemies had harboured for a long time. Finally Louis began to make threatening moves in the area of international trade and commerce. French traders received favourable treatment in Spanish markets at the expense of their English rivals.

In March 1701 a Franco-Spanish naval force was despatched to the West Indies and in October a French company acquired the *asiento*, the exclusive right to the lucrative trade in negro slaves from Africa to the Spanish colonies.

All these measures threatened the interests, either jointly or separately, of the Maritime powers, England and the Dutch Republic, and helped to shift opinion in both countries in favour of war. It is impossible to be sure whether Louis misjudged their desire for peace or whether he cast caution to the wind because he sensed that a major conflict was unavoidable. In either event there must be doubts about Louis's judgment during the year following the publication of Charles II's will. Nevertheless, the united power of France and Spain provided a formidable combination, and we should not assume on the evidence of the disasters ahead that France's position was insupportable from the outset.

France found herself at war on four fronts: in Germany, Spain, the Low Countries and Italy. It was Louis's misfortune that the Captain-General of the Allied armies in the Low Countries, John Churchill, Duke of Marlborough, turned out to be one of the greatest soldiers of the century. He established an unusually close relationship with another distinguished soldier, Prince Eugene of Savoy, who commanded the Emperor's forces, and with Anton Heinsius, the chief spokesman for the United Provinces.

The war went disastrously for France everywhere except in Spain where the Castillians rallied to their new king against the Archduke Charles, the rival claimant who enjoyed the support not only of the Protestant Maritime powers but also of the Castillians' arch-enemies in Spain, the Catalans. Louis's armies were defeated in spectacular pitched battles at Blenheim on the Danube (1704), Ramillies (1706) and Oudenarde (1708) in the Low Countries. Both sides claimed victory in the particularly bloody battle of Malplaquet (1709), north of Maubeuge. By that year the king was desperately seeking peace.

The peace preliminaries of 1709 marked the turning point of the war. Among the sacrifices which Louis was willing to make were the key fortress towns of Ypres, Menin, Furnes, Condé, Maubeuge, Tournai and Lille in the Netherlands, and the great prize of Strasbourg in Alsace. He was also resigned to the expulsion of his grandson from the Spanish Empire. His dream of a united Bourbon bloc in Western Europe was shattered and his policy of building and maintaining security on France's most vulnerable frontiers, accomplished over several generations, lay in ruins. If peace had been signed in 1709 Louis XIV's foreign policy would have ended in disaster and his reputation would have been permanently tarnished. At this critical moment he was inadvertently rescued by the intransigence of the Grand Alliance.

The Allies' problem was Spain. They were unable to achieve a military victory there and were unwilling to allow Louis to make peace without guaranteeing that his grandson would also accept the terms. Clause 4 of the preliminary articles required Louis and the Allies to take concerted action if Philip continued to resist, and clause 37 proclaimed a limited truce between Louis and the Grand Alliance powers during which the frontier fortresses would be handed over. If the truce ended without a settlement in Spain, the Allies would resume the war with the overwhelming advantage of a series of bases from which to conquer France. The Allied demand was for nothing less than unconditional surrender on the part of the Bourbons, with the additional implication that Louis should take up arms against his own grandson. Whether the Allies fully intended the latter, or whether Louis's astute foreign minister, Torcy, deliberately encouraged that interpretation of clause 4 in order to give the king an honourable justification for rejecting the terms, is not clear. But Louis could neither accept such an affront to his family's honour nor sacrifice his country's security by making such momentous concessions. The negotiations therefore broke down and the war continued.

This episode persuaded Louis, prompted by Torcy, who was his most skilful and professional foreign minister, to appeal for support to the French nation. In a letter to his provincial governors, the king insisted that only the excessive demands of his enemies were preventing a peace from being concluded. Significantly the letter made much less of Louis's dynastic link with Spain than of the threat to the country's security. Louis had already recognized the fact that international problems could not be resolved by dynastic methods alone. Now he was beginning to comprehend that guaranteeing the state's security, which was an expensive business in men and money, might ultimately require the support of the nation as well as the agreement of foreign governments. The English had demonstrated that fact by rejecting their king, James II, in 1688 and the Castillians were doing so by obdurately maintaining their support for King Philip V.

The Allies' failure to secure a satisfactory peace in 1709 was the result of their excessive demands. They had learned over many years to distrust and to fear Louis XIV. Having him finally at their mercy, they were determined that he should not threaten them again. He had first demanded unconditional surrender from the Dutch and proceeded to wage war without restraint. Ironically the example which he had given his enemies to emulate saved him from total disaster. Their demands were too extreme to be acceptable, and their quarry subsequently made good his escape.

Later in the year of the abortive negotiations the battle of Malplaquet provided a serious military setback for the Alliance. Shortly afterwards a new Tory government in England embarked upon a peace policy which led to the withdrawal of the English military contingent from Flanders. The Emperor died in 1711, to be succeeded by the Archduke Charles, the Allied candidate for the Spanish Succession. Now it was the Habsburgs rather than the Bourbons who threatened to dominate Europe in a revival of Charles V's Empire, a prospect bound to diminish English and Dutch support for Charles. The French army under Marshal Villars won an important victory at Denain (1712), and France emerged from the Peace of Utrecht (1713–14) with a far more satisfactory settlement than had seemed possible in the dark days of 1709.

The crucial inner ring of fortresses on the Netherlands frontier, Maubeuge, Condé and Lille, which Louis had been resigned to losing in 1709, remained French and so did Strasbourg and Alsace. The security of the frontiers had not been destroyed, and though the Austrian Habsburgs controlled the Southern Netherlands and much of Italy, Louis's grandson remained king of Spain and the Indies. In those areas which most concerned him, the king had escaped from the war with far more success than he deserved. In the area of international trade which interested him only periodically, as at the beginning of the Dutch War and of the War of the Spanish Succession, Louis fared badly. England's colonial grip tightened on North America and the West Indies and her navy controlled the Mediterranean. She acquired the *asiento* which had fleetingly gone to France in 1701. Louis's perspective was, undoubtedly, predominantly continental and military. He could not envisage the global struggles with England that lay ahead.

## CONCLUSION

After the Truce of Ratisbon, Louis XIV's foreign policy became less aggressive. This was primarily because he had built a strong and secure position in Europe which he wished to protect. Nevertheless he was twice more at war before the end of his reign.

There were several reasons for this: the intense mistrust which he had provoked amongst his neighbours; his own miscalculations; and the complex, yet unavoidable issue of the Spanish Succession. Underlying all these factors, however, was the crucial change which was taking place in international relations. Although Louis spoke the language of dynasticism, his actions frequently could only be justified in terms of reason of state. This accounts for the intense hostility and suspicion directed towards him. Earlier generations had accepted the fact that religious differences could provoke savage warfare, with the devastation of land and the destruction of cities. It has become commonplace for later generations to accept such measures and every other means to hand in order to ensure the state's security, whatever the legal or moral objections. Louis, who retained a profound belief in dynastic kingship, was only edging very slowly in this direction. But he was shifting his ground. It appeared to outraged neighbours competing in the complicated game of international relations that, in order to win, the king was changing the rules. For his own part, Louis was beginning to realize in the later years of his reign that national support could be a more effective instrument in international relations than the most legally convincing dynastic claims.

## Epilogue

Louis XIV bequeathed a troubled inheritance to his great-grandson, Louis XV. It was, of course, a fact beyond his control that a series of deaths in the royal family resulted in the succession of a five-year-old child. On the other hand he had done little to modernize the outmoded fiscal system or to loosen the straitjacket of social conservatism, and France would suffer increasingly during the eighteenth century from a lack of flexibility in both these areas. In addition, the religious controversy stirred up by the king's support for the papal bull *Unigenitus* would rage on for half a century after 1715.

The king's reputation declined steadily both at home and abroad from the triumphant times of the early 1680s down to his death in 1715 and beyond. It was in 1680 that the city of Paris honoured him with the title of 'the Great' and the *Collège de Clermont* in the capital was renamed the *Collège Louis-le-Grand*. Yet thirty-five years later in the same city news of his death was greeted with relief and even with enthusiasm. Why should this be so?

The king himself came to recognize that war had played too great a part in his reign, imposing suffering and hardship upon his own subjects and spreading fear amongst his neighbours. It is partly because he left such a deep impression upon Europe that almost three and a half centuries after his accession he continues to attract the attention of historians.

Louis also worked hard at creating his own legend. He understood the importance of political propaganda and we can still see the medals, the statues, the portraits and the palaces which embellished his reign and keep his reputation fresh. He would have been pleased to know that his old home at Versailles attracts millions of visitors a year from all over the world. Under his aegis France became the cultural leader of Europe and foreign princes flattered the king by building palaces in imitation of Versailles.

Louis was one of the architects of modern France. His rule was more professional than that of any of his predecessors. He presided over an emerging state machine which would give far greater power to central government than any dynastic ruler had ever exercised. He also established the shape of France as we know it today. In other words, he achieved secure frontiers. Metz, Toul and Verdun, Alsace, Strasbourg and Franche-Comté, and on the north-east frontier, Maubeuge, Condé and Lille, all lie within the boundaries of the modern French state. As we have seen, he was fortunate to maintain those frontiers at Utrecht. Yet the fact that they still mark France's boundaries to the east is testimony to the significance of Louis XIV's achievement.

# Bibliography

*Place of publication is London unless otherwise stated.*

Two useful bibliographical articles guide the reader to a wide selection of printed material on the reign:

John B. Wolf 'The Reign of Louis XIV: a selected bibliography of writing since the war of 1914–1918', *Journal of Modern History*, XXXVI (1964); and Ragnhild Hatton 'Louis XIV: recent gains in historical knowledge', *Journal of Modern History*, XLV (1973).

The following works in English, several of them containing extensive bibliographical information, cover various aspects of Louis XIV's reign and government:

E. L. Asher, *The Resistance to the Maritime Classes* (Berkeley, 1960).
R. Briggs, *Early Modern France 1560–1715* (Oxford, 1977).
W. E. Brown, *The First Bourbon Century in France* (1971).
W. F. Church, *The Greatness of Louis XIV: myth or reality?* (New York, 1959).
C. W. Cole, *Colbert and a Century of French Mercantilism*, 2 volumes (New York, 1939).
C. W. Cole, *French Mercantilism 1683–1700* (New York, 1943).
Pierre Goubert, *Louis XIV and Twenty Million Frenchmen* (1970).
Ragnhild Hatton, 'Louis XIV: at the court of the Sun King', *The Courts of Europe* (ed. A. G. Dickens, 1977).
Ragnhild Hatton (ed.), *Louis XIV and Absolutism* (1976).
Ragnhild Hatton (ed.), *Louis XIV and Europe* (1976).
Ragnhild Hatton and J. S. Bromley (eds), *William III and Louis XIV: Essays 1680–1720 by and for Mark A. Thomson* (Liverpool, 1968).
H. G. Judge, 'Church and State under Louis XIV', *History,* XLV (1960).
Jacques Levron, *Daily Life at Versailles in the Seventeenth and Eighteenth Centuries* (1968).

Roger Mettam (ed.) *Government and Society in Louis XIV's France* (1977).

Roland Mousnier, *Louis XIV* (Historical Association pamphlet, 1973).

Lionel Rothkrug, *Opposition to Louis XIV. The Political and Social Origins of the French Enlightenment* (Princeton, 1965).

John C. Rule (ed.), *Louis XIV and the Craft of Kingship* (Ohio, 1969).

Thomas J. Schaeper, *The French Council of Commerce, 1700–1715* (Ohio, 1983).

Warren C. Scoville, *The Persecution of the Huguenots and French Economic Development 1680–1720* (Berkeley, 1960).

Paul Sonnino (ed.), *Louis XIV's Mémoires for the Instruction of the Dauphin* (1970).

John B. Wolf, *Louis XIV* (1968).